DISCUSSION PAPER 63

I0122937

# GENDER AND SECURITY IN AFRICA
## An Overview

CHERYL HENDRICKS

NORDISKA AFRIKAINSTITUTET, UPPSALA 2011

*Indexing terms:*
Africa
Conflicts
Women's role
Gender relations
Post-conflict reconstruction
Peacebuilding
Women's participation
Security sector reform
Feminism

Language checking: Peter Colenbrander

ISSN 1104-8417

ISBN 978-91-7106-700-5

© The author and Nordiska Afrikainstitutet 2011

Production: Byrå4

Print on demand, Lightning Source UK Ltd.

# Contents

## Foreword

This Discussion Paper provides a state-of-the-art overview of gender, conflict and security in Africa. It undertakes a review of the literature, main concepts, debates and trends in the field and also identifies the priorities, gaps and areas for further research. In this regard, the paper focuses on gender, conflict and post-conflict reconstruction, and gender and security sector reform in Africa. It engages in a theoretical framing of gender, conflict and post-conflict reconstruction by drawing on feminist perspectives on peace and security, and interrogates gender constructions associated with war, which tend to represent men as protectors and women as in need of protection. This leads to a discussion of the literature on the role(s) of women in arenas of violent conflict or "warscapes." Moving from the broad literature on International Relations, war and peace to studies focusing on Africa, the author provides an overview of the role(s) of women in African arenas of conflict (colonial, postcolonial, and post-Cold War) and evaluates the strengths and weaknesses of existing literature. The nexus between the literature that seeks to lay bare the roles and actions of women in conflict and institutional guidelines and policies is complemented by a critical discussion of the effectiveness of interventions designed to mainstream gender in African peace and security. The paper extends the debate beyond the role of women in conflict and includes their role in peacebuilding and security sector reform. While the paper is critical of perspectives that tend to essentialise the role of women, it notes the importance of such perspectives. The author acknowledges the substantial progress that has been made with regard to research on gender and conflict in Africa, but also points to gaps and areas for further research. The gaps include the absence of substantial research on women in African militaries, women in security sector reform, the impact of peacekeeping missions on gender equality, and the roles of traditional institutions in the perpetuation or transformation of gender relations during and after conflict. In this regard, the author calls for further studies that address the multidimensional and multisectoral aspects of gender, peace and security in Africa. This paper provides a lucid and systematic overview of the literature and perspectives on gender and security in Africa and moves the debate for mainstreaming gender beyond the mere inclusion of more women in security institutions to the imperative of transforming gender relations within those institutions and the processes of post-conflict reconstruction. The paper is an important source of information that will be useful to gender scholars and activists, policy-makers and those with a key interest in African peace and security.

Cyril Obi
Senior Researcher
The Nordic Africa Institute

## Introduction

This paper explores the debates, theoretical perspectives and current trends in gender, conflict and post-conflict reconstruction, and gender and security sector reform (SSR) in Africa. It is underpinned by four key questions: How has the debate about gender, conflict and post-conflict reconstruction evolved? What are the different conceptualisations and assumptions in the literature? How have feminists/gender activists intervened in the debates on SSR? What are the gaps and potential areas for further research? These questions define the scope of the paper and its focus on three broad areas: uncovering women as actors in different battle spaces, women as targets, and the theoretical predilections of gender and conflict. These are not mutually exclusive categories, but provide a heuristic ordering of the core issues in gender and conflict in Africa.

In light of the foregoing, this introductory section involves the broad framing of the theoretical perspectives on gender, conflict and post-conflict reconstruction before zeroing in on Africa. Studies on gender and conflict in Africa have centred on determining the roles that women play during conflict, the gendered constructions of the actors involved in conflict, the impact of conflict on women, reconceptualising security and the ways of addressing gender inequality.

The second section reviews the debates on gender and SSR in Africa. Interventions on gender and SSR are few, particularly by African scholars, and tend to be in the form of practical tools and guidelines aimed at increasing the representation of women in the security sector of African countries. Gender and SSR is a relatively new field of study, largely dominated by practitioners. It is hardly surprising that much of the emphasis has been on developing a rationale for the inclusion of women in the security sector. However, there is increasing recognition of the need to move beyond reducing gender to women and interrogating constructions of men/masculinity and women/femininity as well as the superstructure embedded in the security environment. In the third and concluding section of the paper, existing research gaps and areas for future research are identified.

## Situating the Debates on Gender, Conflict and Post-Conflict Reconstruction

Feminist interventions on peace and security originated among scholars in International Relations, for example, the analyses provided by Cynthia Enloe, V. Spike Peterson, Christine Sylvester and J. Ann Tickner. They challenged (neo)realist representations of war as partial, that is, predominantly representing the experiences of men, and contended that IR assumptions were grounded in an increasingly unviable assertion of the state as the protector. Much of the problem of the invisibility of women in the studies of conflict, they argued, was grounded in

> ... the idea that war is largely fought by men, acting in formal roles as soldiers, that it is defined and contained within a framework of state and seeks to acquire or retain state power. It posits that war is caused by conditions of poverty and frustration and failure of the state; and that while violence against civilians is widespread, it is simply an unfortunate by-product of war. (Martha Thompson 2006:243).

These "state centric and militaristic definitions of security emanated from a masculine bias" that was inbuilt in the then dominant realist theory (Romaniuk 2009:143). The levels of analysis, namely the international system and the state, obfuscated the role of women, as they were predominantly "non-state, anti-state and trans state actors" (Cockburn 2007 citing Spike Peterson and Anne Runyan).

Thus, feminist IR scholars concentrated on exposing the gender constructions associated with war (men as protectors and women in need of protection), on uncovering the varied ways in which women experienced and participated in conflict and posited gender as a central variable in the study of conflict. Hoogensen and Stuvoy (2006) highlighted that gender was a determining factor in deciding "who goes to war and who does not, who is a victim and who is not, and who is legitimate within the security discipline and who is not" (cited in Romaniuk 2009:148).

It is important to note that the work of feminist IR scholars dovetailed with the general rethinking of security in the post-Cold War context. Traditional security paradigms were fast becoming irrelevant in explaining the apparent shift from interstate to intra-state conflicts. The new security paradigm therefore focused on broadening the concept of security to include the referents of security (to the individual) and a widening of the range of actors involved in the provision of security. The human security paradigm, as it became known through the popularisation of the UNDP's 1994 report, drew on Galtung's work on structural violence and redefined security as "freedom from want" and "freedom from fear." The impact of the human security approach was evidenced in policy-making circles as many countries began to incorporate its level of analysis and variables in their security-related strategies towards the developing world, in particular Africa.

Though feminists welcomed the shift from the traditional security paradigm, they also critiqued the limited way in which the approach dealt with gender issues. The *Human Security Now* report was critiqued as "failing to take up women as subjects" (McKay 2004:165); policy-makers were viewed as paying only lip-service to the identification of societal threats, including gender insecurities (Parpart and Thompson 2010), and it was argued that "collapsing femininity or masculinity into the term 'human' could conceal the gendered underpinnings of security practices" (Hudson 2005:157).

The 9/11 terrorist attacks contributed to the displacement of the human security approach under the rubric of anti-terrorism, with a return to perspectives that privileged national or "homeland security agendas." In spite of this, the inadequacies of state-centred analysis have been accepted and both human security and traditional security paradigms coexist, often uncomfortably, within academic and policy-making circles. Many feminists note that although there is an abundance of rhetoric in official documents about the inclusion of gender, the latter remains outside the dominant debates on security and women continue to be absent from the structures for the provision of security. The persistence of this gender gap is partly a reflection of the paradigmatic tensions that reproduce what is privileged and what is not.

The early 1990s was also the period in which peacebuilding, conflict prevention and post-conflict reconstruction became prominent issues on the agenda of the United Nations. The boundaries between conflict prevention, peacebuilding and post-conflict reconstruction are often blurred. There are those who seek to limit peacebuilding to the post-conflict environment, but there are others who view activities aimed at ending the conflict as peacebuilding. Much of the attention in the literature on gender and post-conflict reconstruction has been directed at peacebuilding efforts undertaken by women during conflicts.

The plethora of scholarship and policy-oriented research produced on gender, conflict and post-conflict reconstruction sought to analyse gendered relations in war and peace. The studies focus on the effects of war on women, women's roles as peacebuilders and the consequences of their absence from peace negotiations and peacebuilding processes. Many studies on conflict and peacebuilding analyse the dominant constructions of femininity, portraying women as victims, weak and essentially peaceful by nature. This has in turn contributed to a burgeoning of interventions showing women as actors in conflicts: they "highlighted women's roles as victims, protestors, promoters and participants" (Blanchard 2003). These focus on women as combatants, sex-slaves, gender-based violence against women, women engaged in peace initiatives at the local level, women in peacekeeping, and the vulnerability of women refugees and internally displaced persons (IDPs).

Attention is also paid to the changed gender relations during conflict and the opportunity that conflicts provide for reconstituting gender relations. Continued violence against women in the post-conflict phase is also part of the focus of studies of women in conflict (Caroline Moser and Fiona Clark 2001; Haleh Afshar and Deborah Eade 2004; the UN Report on Women, Peace and Security 2002). A few studies on the constructions of men and masculinities also began to trickle in discussing why men engage in sexual violence/exploitation during war (Paul Higate 2007; Baaz and Stern 2009).

The global outcry against rape as a "weapon of war" generated an international response culminating in policy and legal frameworks aimed at protecting women in war zones and incorporating them into peace-making, peacekeeping, peacebuilding decision-making institutions and practices (see UN Security Council Resolutions 1325, 1820, 1886, 1888). Most of the policy-oriented work has been geared towards facilitating gender mainstreaming in policies and programmes related to peacebuilding/post-conflict reconstruction.

While women's experiences remain an important subject for studies on gender, conflict and post-conflict reconstruction, rather than the problematisation of gender identities and the consequent gendered relations there is still a concentration by scholars, many of whom first began the analysis of gender and war, on militarism and masculinity, and then on "rethinking the meaning of protection ... to address the problems of world security" (Tickner 1995:50), and on advancing alternative visions for conflict transformation. These theorists contend that the "institution of war is closely related to gender and in particular the construction of masculinity" (Francis 2004a:2).

Cockburn notes that "war as institution is made up of, refreshed by and adaptively reproduced by violence as banal practice in the everyday life of the boot camp and battlefield. Masculinity in its various cultural forms is an important content of that cycle ... masculinity shapes war and war shapes masculinity" (Cockburn 2007:248). The military is an important institution for the reproduction of a particularly violent masculinity. Indeed, militarism is posited as a cause for the wars and its particular expression of violence against women. This body of literature queries the preoccupation of those writing on gender and SSR and on their goal of getting more women into security sector institutions, for it would simply buttress patriarchal institutions – the military cannot be transformed for its very functioning is based on gendered constructions and gendered power relations.

Despite all the work showing the intersection between gender, conflict and post-conflict reconstruction, the dominant literature on conflict, still largely emanating from the West, has not taken feminist and/or gender activists interventions on board. At most, it makes passing reference to women as victims. This is also true of the "new wars" literature (Duffield 2001; Kaldor 2001) and of those writing on conflict in Africa in general (Clapham 1996; Reno 1998; Mkandawire 2008). Parpart and Thompson (2011) note that "economic and political factors continue to be seen as the drivers of conflict" and that "the 'new wars' literature has ignored the impact of masculinity and gendered forces, despite the prominence of young male soldiers and gender based violence." Poverty, the desire for social recognition, access to women, and so forth, should all be factored into accounts of why these "new wars" attract young male recruits and why violence against women has become a hallmark of these wars. Parpart and Thompson explain that rape in these conflicts is a "site for performing masculinity" and "reaffirming heteronormativity." Though Zeleza in the edited collection, *The Roots of African Conflicts,* applies a gendered lens to conflicts in Africa and critiques the "new wars" literature, the contributors to this two volume series appear largely oblivious to the question of gender (Hendricks 2008)

The foregoing analyses and conceptualisations of gender and conflict are also pronounced in, and are often drawn from, examinations of African conflicts.

## Gender, Conflict and Post-conflict Reconstruction in Africa

In *Researching Conflict in Africa*, Elisabeth Porter et al. note that research on conflict has been preoccupied with "explanations of the deterioration of the conflict situation and the management of the conflict." Those focusing on the causes emphasise the "contradictions of globalization and the attendant intensification of identity-based struggles for control of power and resources, contradictions of simultaneous economic and political reforms, difficulties in transition, flawed democratization, declining state capacities and diminishing resources and the proliferation of small arms" (2005:2). Much of this research is gender blind. The chapter by Erin Baines, however, reflects on gender research in divided societies and highlights the managerial response to gender. Baines contends that the gender audits and gender-sensitive programmes pay little attention to methods and ethics and "obscure complex dynamics within the violently divided societies such as wider political and economic contexts but also intersections of ethnicity, age or class and gender" (Baines 2005:140).

Over the last 20 years, feminists and gender activists have made a concerted effort to put gender on the agenda of the debates, literature and policy frameworks dealing with conflict and post-conflict reconstruction in Africa. They have portrayed women as actors; described and analysed how and why women are targeted, their vulnerabilities and strengths; made the case for women's inclusion in conflict-prevention, peacemaking and peacebuilding; and provided insights into how to transform gender relations and/or dismantle patriarchy. For the purpose of this overview, the paper has categorised this immense body of literature into three: uncovering women as actors in different battle spaces; women as targets; and the theoretical debates on gender and conflict.

### 1) Uncovering Women in Different Battle Spaces

The battle spaces (arenas of conflict) referred to here are divided into the precolonial, colonial and postcolonial periods. The central focus of this literature was on locating the roles of women in security institutions and conflict. For the precolonial era, the emphasis was on finding women warriors in army formations, e.g., Dahomey, the Monomotapa empire, and so forth. This was part of an effort to debunk the myths about women's place in precolonial African societies.

Much of the early literature concentrated on the colonial period, analysing the role of women in national liberation armies and national liberation struggles. Women were recast as combatants and activists. Urdang's study, *And Still they Dance*, of women in Mozambique's national liberation struggle; Lyons's *Guns and Guerilla Girls*, on women combatants in Zimbabwe; Wilson's, *The Challenge Road: Women and the Eritrean Revolution*; Zerai's, 'Organising women within a national liberation struggle: The case of Eritrea'; Na'Amat Isa's, "The role of women in the Oromo National liberation struggle"; Minale's, "Women and Warfare in Ethiopia"; Becker's, *Namibian Women's Movement,* Hassim and Cock and others on women in South Africa's national liberation struggle and many others writing on countries such as Algeria, Kenya and the Sudan all belong to this genre. The objective was often twofold: to explore women's roles as actors, often taking on roles associated with men; and showing how women are then "put back in their place" after independence. This showed that the gains made during the national liberation struggle were not translated into gender equality in the post-independence period, primarily because the national or racial struggle was seen as paramount. Indeed, South African women's insistence on ensuring that gender equality formed part of the provisions of the new constitution drew on the hindsight of women who had been engaged in the liberation struggles of other countries.

The third battle space is the civil/"uncivil" wars of the post-Cold War period. This body of literature, whether descriptive, theoretical or policy-oriented/managerial, illustrates the varied ways in which women participated in conflicts and peacebuilding. Meredeth Turshen and Clotilde Twangiramariya's *What Women Do in Wartime* (1998) set the scene for the discourse on Africa. They showed that women support war efforts in multiple ways: they resist and fight, are not neutral bystanders during conflict. It is also noted that they sometimes fight among themselves. This study sought to break down the binary stereotypes of "active males/passive females," and build on the findings of previous work examining the "vulnerability of internally displaced or refugee women as victims of war and women's testimonies of their experiences of conflict" (Moser and Clark 2001:4). In *Victims, Perpetrators or Actors?* Moser and Clark further explore this theme to provide a "more comprehensive, global understanding of the complex roles, responsibilities and interests of women and men … to provide a holistic gendered analysis of the agency and identity of women and men throughout violent conflicts" (2001:4).

The work of Meintjes, Pillay and Turshen, *The Aftermath: Women in Post-Conflict Transformation* (2002) was seminal in capturing the different roles of women in violent conflict in Africa. It dwelled on problematising the identities and roles of women in conflict and post-conflict transformation and for setting areas for future research engagement. The authors were of the view that women were not an "undifferentiated category" – their experiences differ and their connections to the conflicts differ. In the chapter by Sheila Meintjes, it is argued that "women have been camp followers for centuries, provisioning armies with food supplies. In modern wars, women have played important roles on the war front in terms of intelligence gathering, communication and transport in addition to providing nursing services" (2002:63). The authors also illustrate how conflict presents an opportunity for women to assume leadership roles in different spaces, for example in the home and IDP camps. Though the extent of the transformation of gender relations during conflict is now questionable and women seem to take up their gender-ascribed roles in the post-conflict phase, the authors provide new insights into the gendered dynamics of conflict.

Though many now critique these early interventions as being centred on women rather than gender, they were important contributions during a period when little was known about the role of women and when women's participation in conflict was being dismissed, often with material consequences, since they were overlooked in disarmament, demobilisation and reintegration programmes. Though the study of gender and conflict has moved on, there continues to be a focus on unearthing women's roles during conflict. This is a theme that can be gleaned in the writings of the following authors: Maria Nzomo, "Gender, Governance and Conflicts in Africa" (2002); Gisela Geisler, *Women and the Remaking of Politics in Southern Africa* (2004), Ernest Harsch, "Women: Africa's ignored combatants" (2005), and Isiaka Badmus, "Explaining women's role in West Africa's Tragic Triplets" (2009).

Examining women's role in liberation movements and rebel armies was matched by an equivalent preoccupation with analysing their role as peacebuilders. Ruth Ochieng's, "The Scars on Their Minds … And their Bodies: The Battle Ground: Women's roles in post-conflict reconstruction" (2002), in addition to looking at the impact of war on women, discussed how women and girls coped during war. It also describes the peacebuilding actions they undertook, highlighting Betty Bigombe's attempts to get Joseph Kony to the peace table; local women negotiating for peace with their sons, brothers and husbands; and the various organisations formed to support women survivors, including the role of Isis-Wicce (Women's International Cross Cultural Exchange) itself in documenting these peace initiatives.

There are several articles on women peacebuilders in Northern Uganda, which has become a laboratory for this type of work as a result of the valuable documentation process conducted by Isis-Wicce. Becker examines the role of Namibian women in peacebuilding and conflict resolution and Josephine Ndayiziga focuses on the role of Burundian women in the peaceful settlement of conflicts. Nadine Puechguirbal and Paul Higate analyse the role of role of women in conflict resolution in Burundi, Democratic Republic of Congo (DRC),

Liberia and Sierra Leone, while Kemi Ogunsanya's *Women transforming conflicts in Africa*, and the workshop reports by the Centre for Conflict Resolution and by the Institute for Security Studies on Women and Peace Building in Africa show the initiatives taken by women at the local level and in traditional societies. They also shed light on women's organisations that were established across Africa to promote peace and to address the continued exclusion of women from the peace negotiation tables.

Many writing on the topic continue to essentialise women as peaceful and illustrate how women draw on their feminine roles to get men to lay down arms. They call for women to be included in peacemaking and peacebuilding activities, stressing their right to be included and their ability to reflect the unique and/or differentiated interests of women. Heidi Hudson notes that according to the critics, the discourse on women and peacebuilding "is enshrined within a neo-liberal managerialist or problem-solving approach which is essentially state-centric and follows a relatively narrow approach to security. In other words women are added to the peacebuilding discourse and the many ambivalent gender voices and power relations are left unexamined" (Hudson 2006:5).

There has been virtually no focus (except to a limited extent in South Africa) on what the few women who have been at the peace tables have actually done to transform gender relations. Peace agreements, whether women have participated in them or not, now routinely acknowledge gender equality. In addition, the provision of a quota for representation by women in decision-making in peace agreements is no guarantee that it will be implemented, as the DRC example shows.

There is a marked absence of research on women in conventional militaries, the police or correctional services in Africa, and that which does exist is predominantly focused on the South African Defence Force and the South African National Defence Force (Cock 1994, 1989, 1997; Heinecken and van der Waag-Cowling 2009; Vaselek and Hendricks 2010). The Geneva-based Centre for the Democratic Control of Armed Forces (DCAF) is also undertaking a study of women in the security sector in West Africa, but in general we know very little about the numbers of women and their experiences and challenges within this sector. We know a bit more about women as peacekeepers. In the context of efforts to implement UN Security Council Resolution 1325, there has been a focus on women peacekeepers within the security sector, but again the focus has been skewed towards South African peacekeepers (Hudson 2000; Pillay 2006; Schoeman 2010). The growing literature on women and peacekeeping is centred on counting the numbers of women deployed and highlighting the special attributes that women bring to peace missions, such as being role models for the local population, dealing with women's issues, being interlocutors and/or curbing tendencies towards sexual excess among their male counterparts. But as Barnes and Olonisakin (2010) and many others indicate, "there is a lack of empirical evidence of the impact of peacekeeping missions and UNSCR 1325 in advancing gender equality at the various national, regional and international levels."

## 2) Women as targets

Scholarly research and reports showing the extent to which women are targeted during conflicts, the reasons for their victimisation and the impact that violent conflict has on the livelihoods, health and dignity of women, is abundant. This literature also emphasises the need for women's inclusion in mediation missions and peace negotiations so that their experiences and needs can be factored into post-conflict reconstruction agendas.

A large proportion of the literature, which emanates mostly from the NGO and international community, focuses on sexual violence, forced marriages/sex-slaves, forced impregnation, mutilation of body parts, killings, large-scale displacement, and so forth (see, for example, the UN Secretary General's report on Women, Peace and Security 2002; the BRIDGE report on Gender and Armed Conflict 2003; and the DCAF report on Sexual Violence in Armed Conflict). The dominant depiction of women in this literature continues to be that of victim.

Explanations of why rape or gender-based violence is pervasive during conflict have also occupied many theorists and show the different nuances in the understanding of the intersection between gender and conflict. These explanations range from the nature of guerilla warfare, where rebels no longer see the need to get the support of the rural populace but instead focus on striking fear into the minds of inhabitants to ensure their compliance. Thus, they target the women. It is also argued that fighters see the need to embarrass men from the opposing camp and show them up as not being able to provide protection. Some explanations about violence against women present it as part of a process of ethnic cleansing, noting also that women are rendered vulnerable during conflict to discourses on masculinity and militarism.

Maria Baaz and Maria Stern's (2009) intervention on this issue is new in the sense that they seek the perpetrators' views on why they rape. They analyse the motivations proffered by the soldiers operating in the DRC. The authors contend that "soldiers' testimonies resonate with understandings of militarized rape in other global contexts," but also "complicate these explanations" (2009:497). The lack of financial resources, ostensibly needed to woo women, was the dominant explanation given by the soldiers for the actions of their colleagues/and possibly themselves. They conclude that with regard to the DRC, soldiers' involvement in rape serves "as a performative act that functions to reconstitute their masculinity – yet simultaneously symbolizes their failure to do so. Through the act of rape several key components of both the provider and the fighter are realized: the sexual relief 'necessary' for the fighter is achieved and the dominance and the heterosexuality of the provider are experienced, however temporarily" (2009:514).

The consequences of gender-based violence and the impact of war on women's lives have been extensively elaborated upon. These include the breakdown of the social setting, trauma, infections, reproductive complications, HIV/AIDs, unwanted pregnancies, women being cast out, poverty, etc. (Karame 2004; Ochieng 2001, 2002; Amalo and Odwee n.d.). Sheila Meintjes et al. (2002) noted that "rapists strip women not only of their economic assets but also their political assets which are their virtue and their reputation." Moreover they went on to show that "men use violence against women and women's fear of violence to reinforce their hold on women." Their work made an interesting observation on the role that customary regimes begin to play in reasserting male dominance, but did not sufficiently expand on it.

During conflict, the justice system is often the first casualty and traditional forms of organisation often re-emerge to fill the vacuum created by the absence of security and justice providers. There has been a focus on the gender discrimination that customary law perpetuates, but no discernable focus on gender, customary law and conflict. The roles that traditional institutions play during conflict to re-establish/reconstruct gender relations have not been adequately studied. Moreover, in the post-conflict environment these traditional institutions often find a new lease on life as traditional justice mechanisms are resurrected and post-conflict reconstruction programmes rely on them to fulfill certain local government functions. This may begin to give more insight into why the "ideological basis underpinning gender relations appear to remain unchanged or even reinforced" (Bushra 2003:258) both during conflict and in the post-conflict environment, despite the roles that women take on during conflict and the political representation gains they make in the reconstituted state.

## 3) Theoretical predilections

The foregoing literature is mainly descriptive. There has been an attempt by a few African scholars to unpack this literature and categorise it into dominant feminist perspectives. There are also important feminist interventions on gender and human security, gender and militarism and gender mainstreaming. Vincent (2003) provides an insightful analysis of the discourse on the role of women in conflict prevention and conflict transformation. She divides the literature into three schools of thought – the liberal pluralist impulse, standpoint feminism and post-structuralism.

The liberal pluralist perspective asserts that women have a particular interest in peace – they are "viewed as having suffered the most from war and therefore have the greatest interest in ending it." They are depicted as mothers, wives, grandmothers, lovers of soldiers and so forth. They thus have a right to representation, and processes (peace-making and post-conflict reconstruction) that do not include them will not be sustainable (Vincent 2003).

But, Vincent argues, there is more to this in the arguments made by women. She notes that:

> Rather than simply postulating that women's voices should be included because they are an interest in society that is important and has unjustifiably been excluded with unfortunate consequences, there appears to be implied in many versions of this discourse something far-reaching. Rather than one valid perspective among many, there is the idea underlying much of what is said that women's perspective is THE perspective that is needed. Women's perspectives are not just held as one among many valid ideas but rather are implicitly viewed as offering a better, more peaceful way of ordering social life, a better way of seeing conflict, its roots and causes and thus a better way of solving it …
> (2003:7)

They also leave out notions of power, race and gender. Hudson (2006) reiterates this point, noting that "the liberal-feminist paradigm produces a hegemonic universalism through its pursuit of the norm of equality (women being like men)."

Standpoint feminism, according to Vincent, claims that theories or practices have been inadequate because they have failed to take into account the "standpoint, activities and experiences of women." To "correct gender blindness it is necessary to identify a set of experiences, activities as well as patterns of thinking, feeling and acting which can be characterized as female" and to make these visible (2003:7). It thus reproduces a "binary universalism" – "men as dominating and violent, women as subordinate and peaceful mothers" (Hudson 2006:6).

Vincent then advocates post-structuralism, which she sees as a "non-essentialist view of politics" where "the social agent is conceived of as constituted by a multiplicity of subject positions whose articulation is always precarious and temporary" (2003:8). This is a perspective that sees identities as being socially constructed. But Hudson does not accept this perspective, instead maintaining that "postmodernist feminist views prioritise special interests over general interest" and that "an overreliance on difference could in turn encourage relativism, political fragmentation and a weakening of the feminist emancipatory agenda" (Hudson 2006:6). Instead, Hudson makes the case for African feminism: "As hybrid manifestations, African feminism acknowledges their connections with international feminism but demarcates a specific African feminism with specific needs and goals arising out of the concrete realities of African women's lives" (2006:6). Within African feminism, the importance of family and cooperation with men to achieve gender equality seem to be paramount.

These have been mainly theoretical debates in the literature and rarely filter into the policy-making perspectives, save for the notion (though often rhetorical) that a gender perspective (power relations between men and women) must foreground the prescriptions. They are, however, important, for how we view women and gender identities (essentialised or constructed) informs the type of responses that bureaucrats devise.

In concluding this section, the paper touches on other theoretical interventions that do not necessarily seek to classify but rather address issues regarding our conceptualisation of security and how it is to be achieved. Hudson's earlier work "A Feminist Reading of Security in Africa" (1998) and Lewis's "Rethinking Human Security: Implications for Gender Mainstreaming" (2006) made important critiques of the human security debate in Africa. Hudson provided a *tour de force* on the evolution of the human security paradigm, feminist critiques of IR and the study of conflict, and sought to "offer an alternative vision of security through the lens of gender," noting that the "security of all people is linked to the security of the women in the continent." She argued for the need to reconceptualise security to include all forms of violence, as they are all interrelated. As such, patriarchy then, too, is conceptualised as a form of violence. Hudson (1998) identified the sources of insecurity for women as culture or customary law, religion, economic factors and the omnipotent culture of the military.

Lewis (2006: 11), building on the work of Hudson, noted that:

> … a perspective that takes into account gender-based violence unmasks the limited understandings of human security, and involves introducing new contexts, concepts and relationships into the human security discourse. Integrating human security work with gender-based violence, whether in the form of research, networking or advocacy, would involve institutes and centres networking with women's organisations (i.e. networking at the local level, rather than solely in terms of inter-agency or inter-state collaboration, or through the high-profile, international networking on which many security studies centres seem to concentrate). Or it would involve systematically addressing studies of gender-based violence (studies which shift the emphasis of politics to the personal, the immediate, the everyday, and away from what is large-scale, national and momentous). And, this, in view of the origin of human security in emphatically masculine and state-centric political studies or security studies, would entail a significant paradigm shift.

A shift to the micro-level, to the "everyday experiences of oppression and fear," and a multidisciplinary approach was needed. Lewis, furthermore, asserted that "gender cannot be examined in isolation, that it is always enmeshed in layers and histories of power and injustice" (Lewis 2006:13). Despite employing the term human security, theorists still predominantly focus on state security, whether in the form of national/regional threat perceptions or the providers of security. At most, women are an add-on.

The theoretical intervention on masculinity and militarism, though on the margins, is still the most virulent critique of the study on gender, conflict and post-conflict reconstruction in Africa. Cock (1991, 1994, 1997, 2001) examines South Africa's war culture and looked at women's roles in the military and liberation armies at the time of the democratic transition and the post-apartheid era. Amina Mama (1998, 2001, 2008) at first analyses gender discourses and militarism in Nigeria and later theorises the relationship more closely, and inserts notions of masculinity and militarism into African feminist discourse. Thus, both Cock and Mama examine the power relations between men and women and the constructions of masculinity and femininity that are central to warfare and its associated institutional expressions. Within warscapes, women are cast in the role of the protected and defended, men as the protectors whose manliness is essentialised through militancy. Mama asserts that the "military man exemplifies the masculine ideal" (1998:4). Militarisation thus "uses and maintains the ideological constructions of gender" (Cock 1994). It is not confined to the barracks such that it produces societies in which violence and domination is normalised, the hierarchical male dominated spaces replicated and the values and norms associated with gender constructions entrenched: patriarchy informs militarism and militarism reinforces patriarchy.

Cock's study of women of the South African military (pre-1994) showed that women were largely in supportive roles, their exclusion from combat based primarily on prevailing stereotypes of the attributes of women and their place in society. Thus incorporation into the military "does not eliminate the subordination of women or even erode patriarchal authority relations … it does not breach the ideology of gender roles" (Cock 1994:154). This seemed to be coming through in Baaz and Stern's paper on *Why do soldiers rape?* too, when they indicate that "constructing the zone of commanding and combat as masculine (and fundamentally heterosexual) required making sense of women's presence in this space in a manner that did not threaten the main logic upon which this notion of masculinity and male heterosexuality depended. The soldiers therefore recast women soldiers as either 'masculine' or as unworthy, devalued feminine" (2009:505). Mama also discounted the ability of the presence of women to fundamentally change the security institutions: "The available evidence suggests that it takes more than one or two, or even a 30% change in personnel to transform the gendered culture and functioning of our more enduring organizational forms" (2001).

Countering the dominant trend of advocating for more women in security institutions, such as the military, they advocate for a transformative project of demilitarisation in which new gender ideologies are formulated, the meaning of security rethought to include a gendered perspective and the place of the military in society interrogated.

Another theoretical intervention currently making inroads is the critique, encapsulated in Hudson's work, of the gender mainstreaming approach (Hudson 2009). She argues that the literature on gender mainstreaming can be divided into two models, namely, an integrative and agenda-setting model. The former seeks to incorporate women into existing policy frameworks while the latter seeks to transform the frameworks and is directed at changing culture, structure and behaviour. Hudson, disillusioned by the trend in gender mainstreaming, contends that it has become "tokenistic gestures in the context of a thriving gender mainstreaming industry complete with gender advisors, workshops handbooks and toolkits." There is a conflation of gender and women in gender mainstreaming and therefore the focus has been on gender balance rather than transforming gender relations. Hudson is aware of the critique leveled against theorists of not providing concrete policy solutions, but retorts that "gender mainstreaming may offer greater visibility for women in the political sphere, but if women's participation remains confined to liberal individualist ideology which is not representative of women's experiences at the grassroots level, gender relations stay untransformed" (Hudson 2009).

Clearly policy-makers, gender advisors and experts and academics are not on the same page as to what must be done. This is primarily because their imperatives are different – the former need to make quick gains in spaces that are difficult to transform, so their focus is on inclusion, while the latter seek to understand and generate knowledge and are afforded the space to be critically reflexive and to advocate for longer-term transformational strategies.

Anderlini best captured all the tensions raised above when she posed the question of how we bring a feminist discourse on militarisation and the human security discourse into the realm of policy-making and implementation. Drawing on South Africa's experience, she argues:

> … that at least the first part of this is possible, i.e. when you have feminist women engaged in security issues, they can, and have, influenced the policy discourse and reshaped national priorities. But the question of implementation is more thorny – at a conceptual level it's possible to talk about human security as the core value determining a nation's security agenda – but at the point of implementation you come face to face with more difficult things ranging from dealing with vested interest groups to the problem of how do you balance efforts to promote human security at a structural level, with more immediate problems of gun violence (resulting from conflict or post conflict) and the reflex to use standards, tried and trusted methods of dealing with problems (comment made in the INSTRAW E-Discussion 2004).

This overview of the literature on gender, conflict and post-conflict reconstruction indicates, despite its relative infancy, the substantial research into and analyses of these issues in the African context. It points to the conceptual growth and the strengths and limitations of the analyses and to how differing perspectives coexist, at times reinforcing each other and at times totally at odds. Uncovering women as actors on the battlefields was a necessary precursor to interrogating their gendered constructions in these spaces. Showing how women are targeted during conflict informed studies of the construction of masculinity. Also, highlighting the absence of women from peace settlements underscored the need for gender mainstreaming if a sustainable peace for all is to be achieved. With hindsight, it is easy to point to the shortcomings of essentialist interpretations, but, the literature should be read as a whole and as complementary, rather than in a dismissive and intellectually arrogant manner.

## Gender and Security Sector Reform

SSR is a relatively recent entry into the debates on gender and security. The OECD DAC Handbook views SSR as a process "which includes all the actors, their roles, responsibilities and actions – working together to manage and operate the system in a manner that is more consistent with democratic norms and sound principles of good governance, and thus contributes to a well-functioning security framework" (2007). The Global Facilitation Network for Security Sector Reform (GFN-SSR) Guide for beginners, notes that "SSR aims to create a secure environment that is conducive to development, poverty reduction, good governance and in particular the growth of democratic institutions based on the rule of law" (2007). SSR is posited as being "transformative," "holistic," and as making the link between security and development. Theoretically it is grounded in the human security paradigm, promoting values of democratisation, legitimacy, people-centredness, local ownership, inclusion and diversity and foregrounding the security of both the state and its citizens. It seeks to create an accountable, effective and efficient security sector through a set of reforms at the political, institutional, economic and societal levels. It is then little wonder that this system-wide approach to security came to be viewed as the panacea for Africa's security problems.

Since Africa accounts for the majority of the world's post-Cold War conflicts, it has also been the arena for many of the post-conflict SSR programmes. Defence and police have primarily been the beneficiaries/targets of these reform processes, with correctional services and intelligence receiving very little attention. Despite the participation of women in the liberation and rebel armies, very few were included in Africa's postcolonial armies, the reconstituted armies of post-conflict states or were beneficiaries of DDR programmes. In fact, it is hard to obtain any information on how many women actually serve in the militaries in the respective African countries. From the *Military Balance,* we can discern overall force size, equipment and budgets of African militaries, but we are unable to provide data on the number of women in these services, except in a few instances like South Africa, where these were at first readily available. However, even these countries are becoming more secretive about the information.

Although there are a few African women who write on SSR in Africa (see Janine Rauch, Lauren Hutton, Sandy Africa, Vanessa Farr, Funmi Olonisakin, Monica Juma), there is very little scholarly material specifically dealing with gender and SSR. Much of the work on gender and SSR, not necessary by African scholars, is in the form of handbooks, toolkits and conference reports (Pearson Peacekeeping Centre and ECOWAS Roundtable Report 2006, Bastick 2008, ISS Report 2008, Instraw and DCAF Toolkit 2008, GFN-SSR 2009) The works by Clarke (2008), De Klerk (2009) and Vaselek and Hendricks (2010) specifically focus on gender and SSR. The Instraw and DCAF Toolkit on Gender and SSR was the first comprehensive overview on the topic, covering a broad range of institutions with examples of best practices from all over the world: police, defence, justice, penal, border management, parliamentary oversight, national security policy-making, civil society oversight, monitoring and evaluation and gender training for security personnel. It sought to fill the practitioners' gap with guidelines for integrating gender into SSR.

Since the toolkit aimed at providing policy advice, its emphasis was on why and how women needed to be included in the security sector and the opportunity that SSR provided for this accomplishment. The point of departure was that "there is a strong recognition that SSR should meet the different security needs of men, women, boys and girls. The integration of gender issues is also key to the effectiveness and accountability of the security sector and to local ownership and legitimacy of SSR processes" (Jacob, Bendix, Stanley 2008).

Glancing through the individual institutionally-based guides, one gleans that including women:

1. Adheres to international instruments such as the Beijing Declaration, UN Security Council Resolution CR1325 and the Universal Declaration of Human Rights;
2. Increases operational effectiveness: awareness of culturally-specific gender issues will help staff adjust to the host community and be more responsive to the cultural milieu; female operators are needed to conduct searches on women and gather accurate intelligence; local men and women see female staff as more approachable; enhances the capacity to respond to gender-specific needs such as gender-based violence, domestic violence or human trafficking; builds civilian trust;
3. Brings added and specific human resource skills and strengths, e.g., good women have good communication and facilitation skills. Diversity in force composition and gender mainstreaming in multidimensional peace operations enables enhanced performance of these tasks;

4. Promotes non-discrimination in the workplace and creates more representative institutions that mirror the society;
5. Prevents human rights violations;
6. Increases the relevance and sustainability of national security policies;
7. Strengthens accountability; and
8. Maximises their abilities to fulfil their role in protecting societies.

The opportunity for integrating gender issues into the security sector arises during times such as the formulation of peace agreements, participatory national dialogues and constitutional and electoral reform processes (Jacob, Bendix, Stanley 2008).

There have also been a number of reports noting the challenges of incorporating and retaining women in this sector, such as persistent gender biases, lack of educational and training opportunities, lack of a quota system for women, cultural attitudes, safety concerns, family responsibilities, women-unfriendly equipment and uniform design and living quarters, lack of role models and so forth.

The dominant argument made in the literature on gender and SSR for women's inclusion is based on the proposition that women have a right to be in the sector, that they add value and have a unique set of qualities that peace missions can draw on. Their incorporation is not only good for the security sector, for "operational effectiveness," but it is good for the societies as a whole as they create a more responsive security sector, particularly to the needs of women. These arguments seem to shift the onus of human security and gender-responsive security on to the shoulders of women.

Quite predictably, the critique of the above approach has been that women's inclusion is fashioned in an "instrumentalist" way "that treats them either as overlooked beneficiaries (DDR) or as sources of knowledge and skills which will enhance the world of the security structures" (Clarke 2008). The call by feminists would be for a consideration of "deeper transformation of the gender relations that characterize security institutions and systems and addresses questions of hierarchy and masculinity" (Clarke 2008). Clarke, however, notes that at least on paper SSR provides an opportunity to liberate the security sector from its militarised overtones, but doubts whether "gender securocrats" will move the debate beyond a liberal feminist approach.

Valasek and Hendricks (2010) have put forward the case for a more transformative gender and SSR agenda. They argue that "gender roles are at the core of the social discourse on peace and security," but:

> … when faced with the call to reform in the name of gender equality, the most common response from African armed forces and police services has been to step-up the recruitment of female personnel. However, a narrow approach of re-

cruitment reform will only have a minor impact upon the institution as a whole. Without a comprehensive approach, isolated gender initiatives will have little or no impact. Therefore, the integration of gender issues can be a useful indicator to determine whether reforms have been cross-cutting and coherent.

It is easier to include than to transform institutional cultures. In a world where measurable targets have become the norm for performance evaluations and in a sector where gender stereotypes still dominate both the providers and the recipients of security, we are likely to remain at this level of discourse for the foreseeable future. If the debates and practices on gender and SSR have not lived up to expectations, they are mirroring the growing disillusionment with SSR as a whole. For despite the reforms to the security sector, African societies remain violent and vulnerable spaces for both men and women.

## So what? Where are the gaps?

The approaches to gender and conflict vary from the simplistic and essentialistic to the nuanced and constructed identity representations that are central to gendered power relations.

There are still gaps in terms of the prevailing explanations for the disjuncture between policy formulation, implementation and a continued patriarchal system in which women remain disproportionally affected by conflict and general violence. The gaps point to a need for more empirical work on monitoring and evaluation of existing policies and programmes in Africa. We need to begin to collate data on the experiences of women and document and analyse the contributions of women who have been part of peace negotiations, peace missions, security-related parliamentary portfolio committees, and the few who have made it to the upper levels of security institutions.

There is also a need to collate basic data on the number of women in the security sector in Africa and establish whether or not they view their own contributions in the ways presented in the literature. We need to discern how these women, often marginalised by other gender equality activists, organise themselves within these security institutions and what effect this has in terms of transforming institutional cultures and providing more gender-responsive security rather than presuming that nothing has been done and that outside intervention is therefore necessary to transform the "last bastion of male dominance." More empirical evidence is also required to explain the ways in which women in conflict zones protect themselves. This is also relevant to how women in other spaces access security and the implications of this for the ways in which security is currently framed and provided.

The relationship between customary institutions and gender, peace and security has not received adequate attention. It is therefore necessary to interrogate what transformational institutional change in the security sector encompasses and ways in which this can be achieved. Last but not least, there is a need to document country- and security sector-specific case studies on gender and SSR in Africa to highlight and compare processes and outcomes across time and space. Therefore, a lot remains to be done to gain a more comprehensive insight into the multidimensional and multisectoral aspects of gender, peace and security in Africa.

# References

Afshar, H., 2003, "Women and Wars: Some trajectories towards a feminist peace," *Development in Practice,* Vol. 13, No. 2/3, pp 178–88.

Afshar, H. and D. Eade, 2004, *Development, Women and War: Feminist Perspectives.* Oxford: Oxfam.

Amalo, C. and J. Odwee, n.d., "Sexual and Gender-Based Violence against women in conflict areas in Uganda: A case of Kitgum District." Unpublished paper.

Anderlini, S., 2004, "Gender and SSR," Summary of E-discussion 4 Oct–7 November. Instraw.

Andunga, M., 1997, "Women and Warfare in Ethiopia: A case study of their role during the campaign of Adwa 1895–96." Addis Ababa: Organisation for Social ScienceReseach in Eastern and Southern Africa (OSSREA).

Baaz, M. and M. Stern, 2009, " Why do Soldiers Rape? Masculinity, Violence and Sexuality in the Armed Forces in the DRC," *International Studies Quarterly,* Vol. 53, pp. 495–518.

Badmus, I., 2009, "Explaining Women's roles in West Africa's Tragic Triplet: Sierra Leone, Liberia and Côte d'Ivoire," *Journal of Alternative Perspectives in the Social Sciences,* Vol. 1, No. 3.

Baines, E., 2005, "Gender research in violently divided societies: Methods and ethics of 'international' researchers in Rwanda," in Porter, E. et al. (eds), *Researching Conflict in Africa: Insights and Experiences.* Tokyo: United Nations University Press.

Bastick, M., 2008, "Integrating gender in post-conflict security sector reform," in *SIPRI Yearbook.* Geneva: DCAF.

Bastick, M., K. Grimm and R. Kunz, 2007, *Sexual Violence in Armed Conflict: Global Overview and Implications for the Security Sector.* Geneva: DCAF.

Bastik, M. and K. Valasek (eds), 2008, *Gender and SSR Toolkit.* Geneva: DCAF, OSCE/ODIHR/UN-INSTRAW.

Becker, H., 2003, "Women, Politics and Peace in Northern Namibia," in *Women and Peace in Africa: Case Studies in Traditional Conflict Resolutio.* Paris: UNESCO.

—, 1995, *Namibian Women's Movement 1980 to 1992: From anticolonial resistance to reconstruction.* Frankfurt/Main: Iko.

Blanchard, E., 2003, "Gender, International Relations, and the Development of a Feminist Security Theory," *Signs,* Vol. 28, No. 4, pp. 1289–1312.

Centre for Conflict Resolution, 2005, "Women and Peacebuilding in Africa." Seminar Report – Conference hosted in Cape Town, 27–28 October.

Clapham, C., 1996, African Guerillas. Cambridge: Cambridge University Press.

Clarke, Y., 2008, "Security Sector Reform in Africa: A Lost Opportunity to Deconstruct Militarised Masculinities," *Feminist Africa,* Issue 10, pp. 49–66.

Cock, J., 1989, "Keeping the Fires Burning: Militarisation and the Politics of Gender in South Africa," *Review of African Political Economy,* No. 45/46, Militarism, Warlords and the Problems of Democracy.

—, 1991, *Colonels and Cadres: War and Gender in South Africa.* Cape Town: Oxford University Press.

—, 1994, "Women in and the Military: Implications for Demilitarisation in the 1990's in South Africa," *Gender and Society,* Vol. 1, No. 2, pp. 152–69.

—, 1997, "The Feminist Challenge to Militarism" in *Agenda,* No. 36, pp. 27–39.

—, 2001, "Closing the Circle: Towards a gendered understanding of war and peace," African Gender Institute, University of Cape Town, Newsletter, Vol. 8.

Cockburn, C., 2007, *From Where We Stand. War, Women's Activism and Feminist Analysis.* London: Zed Books.

De Klerk, L.M., 2010, "Democracy and the People: Gender and Security in Post-Conflict South Africa." Unpublished paper.

De Waal, A., 2001, *Who Fights? Who Cares?* Trenton NJ: Africa World Press.

Duffield, M., 2001, *Global Governance and the New Wars: The Merging of Development and Security.* London: Zed Books.

El-Bushra, J., 2003, "Fused in Combat: Gender Relations and Armed Conflict," *Development in Practice,* Vol. 13, No. 2/3, pp. 252–65.

El Jack, A. 2003. "Gender and Armed Conflict: Overview Report." Sussex: BRIDGE (development-gender), Institute of Development Studies (IDS), UK.

Ekiyor, T. and L.M. Wanyeki, 2008, "National Implementation of SCR 1325 (2000) in Africa: Needs Assessment and Plan of Action." New York: Office of the Special Adviser on Gender Issues and Advancement, Department of Economic and Social Affairs, United Nations.

Enloe, C., 1989, *Bananas, Beaches and Bases: Making Feminist Sense of International Politics.* Berkeley CA: University of California Press.

Enloe, C., 1998, "All the Men are in Militias, All the Women are Victims," in Lorentzen, L.A. (ed.), *The Women and War Reader.* New York: New York University Press.

Enloe, C., 2000, *Manoevers: The International Politics of Militarizing Women's Lives.* Berkeley CA: University of California Press.

Farr V., 2006, "Voices from the Margins: A response to 'security sector reform in developing and transitional countries'." Paper for the Berghof Research Centre. http://www.berghof-handbook.net/documents/publications/dialogue2_farr.pdf

Francis, D, 2004a, "Culture, Power Asymmetries and Gender in Conflict Transformation." Berghof Research Centre for Conflict Management. http://www. berghof-handbook.net. pp. 1–15.

—, 2004b, "Gender and Conflict Transformation," Committee for Conflict Transformation Support, Discussion Paper No. 23. http//www.c-r.org/ccts/ccts 23/ gender_conflict_trans.htn.

Geisler, G., 2004, *Women and the Remaking of Politics in Southern Africa: Negotiating Autonomy, Incorporation and Representation.* Uppsala: Nordic Africa Institute.

GFN-SSR, 2009, M. Jacob, D. Bendix and R. Stanley (eds.), "Engendering Security Sector Reform, A Workshop Report," Berlin: Freie Universitat, http://www.ssrnetwork.net/uploaded_files/4534.pdf

—, 2007, "A beginner's guide to security sector reform." www.ssrnetwork.net

Goldstein, J.S., 2001, *War and Gender: How Gender Shapes the War System and Vice Versa.* Cambridge: Cambridge University Press.

Harsch, E., 2005, "Women: Africa's ignored combatants, Gradual progress towards a greater role in DDR," *Africa Renewal,* Vol. 19, No. 3.

Hassim, S., 2006, *Women's Organisations and Democracy in South Africa: Contesting authority.* Madison WI: University of Wisconsin Press.

Heinecken, L. and N. van der Waag-Cowling, 2009, "The Politics of Race and Gender in South Africa Armed Forces; Issues, Challenges and Lessons," *Commonwealth and Comparative Politics,* Vol. 47, No. 4, pp. 517–38.

Hendricks, C., 2008, "Review of The Roots of African Conflicts: The Causes and Costs and the Resolution of African Conflicts," in Nhema, Alfred and Paul Zeleza (eds), *Feminist Africa,* Issue 10.

Hendricks, C. and M. Chivasa, 2009, "Women and Peacebuilding in Africa," Workshop Report. Pretoria: Institute of Security Studies.

Hendricks, C. and K. Valasek, 2010, "Gender and Security Sector Transformation: From theory to South African Practice." *SIPRI Yearbook.* Geneva: DCAF.

Hilgate, P., 2007, "Peacekeepers, Masculinities, and Sexual Exploitation," *Men and Masculinities,* Vol. 10, No. 1, pp. 99–119. http://jmm.sagepub.com

Hoogensen, G. and S. Rottem, 2004, "Gender Identity and the Subject of Security," *Security Dialogue,* Vol. 35, No. 2, pp. 155–71.

Hoogensen, G. and K. Stuvoy, 2006, "Gender, Resistance and Human Security," *Security Dialogue,* Vol. 37, No. 2, pp. 207–28.

Hudson, H., 1998, "A Feminist Reading of Security in Africa," *Caring Security in Africa,* Monograph 20. Pretoria: Institute for Security Studies.

—, 2000, "Mainstreaming Gender in Peacekeeping Operations: Can Africa Learn from International Experience," *African Security Review,* Vol. 9, No. 4.

—, 2005, "Doing Security as though Humans Matter: A Feminist Perspective on Gender and the Politics of Human Security," *Security Dialogue,* Vol. 36, No. 2, pp. 155–74.

—, 2006, "Human Security and Peace-building through a gender lens: Challenges of implementation in Africa." DISS Working Paper No. 2006/37.

—, 2009, "Feminist Theory meets peacebuilding: Policy implications for gender mainstreaming and national action plans." Paper presented at the International Studies Association Conference, New York, February.

Isa, Na'amat, 2008, "The Role of Women in the Oromo National Liberation Movement," *The Sidama Concern.*

Kaldor, M., 2001, "Beyond Militarism, Arms Races and Arms Control." Essay prepared for the Nobel Prize Centennial Symposium, 6–8 December. http://essays.ssrc.org/sept11/essays/kaldor.htm

Kalifani, H., A. Marshall, R. Ochieng and N. Kakembo, 2007, "Experiences of Women War-Torture Survivors in Uganda: Implications for Health and Human Rights," *Journal of International Women's Studies,* Vol. 8, No. 4. pp. 1–17.

Karame, K. (ed), 2004, *Gender and Peace-building in Africa.* Oslo: TfP and NUPI.

Koen, K., 2006, "Claiming space: Reconfiguring women's roles in post-conflict situations." Institute for Security Studies Occasional Paper No. 121.

Lewis, D., 2006, "Rethinking Human Security: The Implications for Gender Mainstreaming," in Hendricks, Cheryl (ed.), *From State Security to Human Security in Southern Africa: Policy Research and Capacity Building Challenges,* Monograph 122. Pretoria: Institute for Security Studies.

Lyons, T., 2004, *Guns and Guerilla Girls: Women in the Zimbabwean Liberation Struggle.* Trenton NJ: Africa World Press.

Mama, A., 1998, "Khaki in the family: Gender discourses and militarism in Nigeria," *African Studies Review,* Vol. 41, No. 2, pp. 1–18.

—, 2001, "Gender in Action: Militarism and War," African Gender Insitute, Univeristy of Cape Town, Newsletter, June.

Mama, A. and M. Okazawa-Rey, 2008, "Editorial: Conflict and Women's Activism," *Feminist Africa,* Issue 10, pp. 1–8.

Marks, R. and T. Denham, 2006, "Roundtable on Police and gendarmerie women in peace operations: West African solutions to gender mainstreaming challenges." Workshop report. Pearson Peacekeeping Centre and ECOWAS.

McKay, S., 2004, "Women, Human Security and Peace-Building: A Feminist Analysis," *Conflict and Human Security: A Search for New Approaches of Peace-building,* IPSHU English Research Report Series No. 19, pp. 152–74.

Meintjies, S., M. Turshen and A. Pillay (eds), 2002, *The Aftermath: Women in Post-Conflict Transformation.* London and New York: Zed Books.

Meintjies, S., 2002, "War and Post war shifts in gender relations," in Meintjes, S. et al. (eds), *The Aftermath: Women in Post-Conflict Transformation.* London and New York: Zed Books.

Mkandawire, T., 2008, "The Terrible Toll of Postcolonial Rebel Movements: Towards an Explanation of the violence against the Peasantry," in Nhema, A. and P.T. Zeleza (eds), *The Roots of African Conflicts: The Management of Conflict Resolution and Post-Conflict Reconstruction.* Addis Ababa: OSSREA.

Moser, C. and F. Clark (ed.), 2001, *Victims, Perpetrators or Actors? Gender, Armed Conflict and Political Violence.* London and New York: Zed Books.

Ntahobari J. and B. Ndayiziga, 2003, "The role of Burundian women in the peaceful settlement of conflicts," in *Women and Peace in Africa: Case Studies on Traditional Conflict Resolution,* Paris: UNESCO.

Nwoye, M., 2009, "Role of women in peacebuilding and conflict resolution in African traditional societies: a selective review." Accessed on http://www.afrikaworld.net/afrel/chinwenwoye.htm

Nzomo, M., 2002, "Gender Governance and Conflict in Africa," unpublished paper, http://unpan1.un.org/intradoc/groups/public/docu…

Ochieng, R.O., 2002, "*The Scars* on Women's *Minds* and Bodies. Women's Roles in Post-Conflict Reconstruction in Uganda". Presented at the 19th International Peace Research Conference, Kyung Hee University, South Korea.

—, 2001, "The Powerless in Search of Peace: Ugandan Women's Experiences of Wars," Africa Gender Institute, University of Cape Town, Newsletter, Vol. 8. accessed at http://web.uct.ac.za/org/agi/pubs/newsletters/Vol 8/Uganda.htm.

OECD, 2007, *OECD DAC Handbook on Security System Reform: Supporting Security and Justice.* Paris: OECD, *http://www.oecd.org/dataoecd/43/25/38406485.pdf*

Ogunsanya, K, 2007, "Women Transforming Conflict in Africa: Descriptive Studies from Burundi, Côte d' Ivoire, Sierra Leone, South Africa and Sudan." ACCORD Occasional Paper Series, Vols. 2/3.

Olonisakin, F., K. Barnes and E. Ikpe (eds), 2011, *Women, Peace and Security: Translating Policy into Practice.* London: Routledge.

Parpart, J. and L. Thompson, 2011, "Engendering African International Relations," in Cornelissen, S., F. Cheru and T. Shaw (eds), *Africa and International Relations Theory in the 21ˢᵗ Century.* Basingstoke: Palgrave Macmillan.

Peterson, V. Spike (ed.), 1992, *Gendered States: Feminist (Re) Visions on International Relations Theory.* Boulder CO: Lynne Rienner.

Pillay, A., 2006, "Gender, Peace and Peacekeeping: Lessons from Southern Africa." Institute of Strategic Studies Occasional Paper 128.

Porter, E., R. Gillian, S. Marie, S. Albrecht S. and E. Osaghae (eds), 2005, *Researching Conflict in Africa: Insights and Experiences.* Hong Kong: United Nations University Press.

Puechgirbal, N., 2004, "Involving women in peace-processes: Lessons from four African countries," in Karame, K. (ed.) 2004, *Gender and Peace-building in Africa.* Oslo: TfP and NUPI.

Rehn, E. and E.J. Sirleaf, 2002, "Women, War and Peace." Independent experts assessment on the impact of armed conflict on women and women's roles in peacebuilding. New York: UNIFEM.

Reno, W., 1998, *Warlord Politics and African States.* Cambridge: Cambridge University Press.

Romaniuk, S., 2009, "Engaging Gender (In) Security," *Gender and Media Diversity Journal,* pp. 143–52.

Schoeman, M., 2010, "South African female peacekeepers on mission in Africa: Progress, challenges and policy options for increased participation." *Policy* Note No. 1. Uppsala: Nordic Africa Institute.

Strickland, R. and N. Duvvury, 2003, "Gender Equity and Peacebuilding: From Rhetoric to Reality: Find the Way." Discussion Paper, ICRW.

Thompson, M., 2006, "Women, gender, and conflict: Making the connections," *Development in Practice*, Vol. 16, No. 3, pp. 342–53.

Tickner, J. Ann., 1992, *Gender in International Relations: Feminist Perspectives on Achieving Global Security*. New York: Columbia University Press.

—, 1995, "Introducing Feminist Perspectives into Peace and World Security Courses," *Women's Studies Quarterly: Rethinking Women's Peace Studies,* Vol. 23, Nos. 3/4, pp. 48–57.

Tshirgi, N, 2003, "Peacebuilding as the link between Security and Development: Is the Window of Opportunity Closing?" International Peace Academy Policy Report.

Turshen, M. and C. Twagiramariya (eds), 1998, *What Women Do in Wartime: Gender and Conflict in Africa*. New York: Zed Books.

UNDP, 1994, *Human Development Report.* New York: Oxford University Press.

UN Commission on Human Security, 2004, *Human Security Now Report.* New York: UNCHS

UN, 2002, "Women, Peace and Security." Study submitted by the Secretary General pursuant to UNSCR 1325.

Urdang, S., 1988, *And Still they Dance: Women, Destabilisation and the Struggle for Mozambique.* New York: Monthly Review Press.

Vincent, L., 2003, "Current Discourse on the Role of Women in Conflict Prevention and Conflict Prevention and Conflict Transformation," ACCORD *Conflict Trends*, Issue 3, pp. 5–10.

Zerai, W., 1994, "Organising women within a national liberation struggle: The case of Eritrea," *Economic and Political Weekly,* 29 October.

# DISCUSSION PAPERS PUBLISHED BY THE INSTITUTE

Recent issues in the series are available electronically for download free of charge
www.nai.uu.se

1. Kenneth Hermele and Bertil Odén, *Sanctions and Dilemmas. Some Implications of Economic Sanctions against South Africa.*
1988. 43 pp. ISBN 91-7106-286-6

2. Elling Njål Tjönneland, *Pax Pretoriana. The Fall of Apartheid and the Politics of Regional Destabilisation.*
1989. 31 pp. ISBN 91-7106-292-0

3. Hans Gustafsson, Bertil Odén and Andreas Tegen, *South African Minerals. An Analysis of Western Dependence.*
1990. 47 pp. ISBN 91-7106-307-2

4. Bertil Egerö, *South African Bantustans. From Dumping Grounds to Battlefronts.*
1991. 46 pp. ISBN 91-7106-315-3

5. Carlos Lopes, *Enough is Enough! For an Alternative Diagnosis of the African Crisis.*
1994. 38 pp. ISBN 91-7106-347-1

6. Annika Dahlberg, *Contesting Views and Changing Paradigms.*
1994. 59 pp. ISBN 91-7106-357-9

7. Bertil Odén, *Southern African Futures. Critical Factors for Regional Development in Southern Africa.*
1996. 35 pp. ISBN 91-7106-392-7

8. Colin Leys and Mahmood Mamdani, *Crisis and Reconstruction – African Perspectives.*
1997. 26 pp. ISBN 91-7106-417-6

9. Gudrun Dahl, *Responsibility and Partnership in Swedish Aid Discourse.*
2001. 30 pp. ISBN 91-7106-473-7

10. Henning Melber and Christopher Saunders, *Transition in Southern Africa – Comparative Aspects.*
2001. 28 pp. ISBN 91-7106-480-X

11. *Regionalism and Regional Integration in Africa.*
2001. 74 pp. ISBN 91-7106-484-2

12. Souleymane Bachir Diagne, et al., *Identity and Beyond: Rethinking Africanity.*
2001. 33 pp. ISBN 91-7106-487-7

13. Georges Nzongola-Ntalaja, et al., *Africa in the New Millennium.* Edited by Raymond Suttner.
2001. 53 pp. ISBN 91-7106-488-5

14. *Zimbabwe's Presidential Elections 2002.* Edited by Henning Melber.
2002. 88 pp. ISBN 91-7106-490-7

15. Birgit Brock-Utne, *Language, Education and Democracy in Africa.*
2002. 47 pp. ISBN 91-7106-491-5

16. Henning Melber et al., *The New Partnership for Africa's development (NEPAD).*
2002. 36 pp. ISBN 91-7106-492-3

17. Juma Okuku, *Ethnicity, State Power and the Democratisation Process in Uganda.*
2002. 42 pp. ISBN 91-7106-493-1

18. Yul Derek Davids, et al., *Measuring Democracy and Human Rights in Southern Africa.* Compiled by Henning Melber.
2002. 50 pp. ISBN 91-7106-497-4

19. Michael Neocosmos, Raymond Suttner and Ian Taylor, *Political Cultures in Democratic South Africa.* Compiled by Henning Melber.
2002. 52 pp. ISBN 91-7106-498-2

20. Martin Legassick, *Armed Struggle and Democracy. The Case of South Africa.*
2002. 53 pp. ISBN 91-7106-504-0

21. Reinhart Kössler, Henning Melber and Per Strand, *Development from Below. A Namibian Case Study.*
2003. 32 pp. ISBN 91-7106-507-5

22. Fred Hendricks, *Fault-Lines in South African Democracy. Continuing Crises of Inequality and Injustice.*
2003. 32 pp. ISBN 91-7106-508-3

23. Kenneth Good, *Bushmen and Diamonds. (Un) Civil Society in Botswana.*
2003. 39 pp. ISBN 91-7106-520-2

24. Robert Kappel, Andreas Mehler, Henning Melber and Anders Danielson, *Structural Stability in an African Context.*
2003. 55 pp. ISBN 91-7106-521-0

25. Patrick Bond, *South Africa and Global Apartheid. Continental and International Policies and Politics.*
2004. 45 pp. ISBN 91-7106-523-7

26. Bonnie Campbell (ed.), *Regulating Mining in Africa. For whose benefit?*
2004. 89 pp. ISBN 91-7106-527-X

27. Suzanne Dansereau and Mario Zamponi, *Zimbabwe – The Political Economy of Decline.* Compiled by Henning Melber.
2005. 43 pp. ISBN 91-7106-541-5

28. Lars Buur and Helene Maria Kyed, *State Recogni-tion of Traditional Authority in Mozambique. The nexus of Community Representation and State Assist-ance.* 2005. 30 pp. ISBN 91-7106-547-4

29. Hans Eriksson and Björn Hagströmer, *Chad – Towards Democratisation or Petro-Dictatorship?* 2005. 82 pp.ISBN 91-7106-549-

30. Mai Palmberg and Ranka Primorac (eds), *Skinning the Skunk – Facing Zimbabwean Futures.* 2005. 40 pp. ISBN 91-7106-552-0

31. Michael Brüntrup, Henning Melber and Ian Taylor, *Africa, Regional Cooperation and the World Market – Socio-Economic Strategies in Times of Global Trade Regimes.* Com-piled by Henning Melber. 2006. 70 pp. ISBN 91-7106-559-8

32. Fibian Kavulani Lukalo, *Extended Handshake or Wrestling Match? – Youth and Urban Culture Celebrating Politics in Kenya.* 2006.58 pp. ISBN 91-7106-567-9

33. Tekeste Negash, *Education in Ethiopia: From Crisis to the Brink of Collapse.* 2006. 55 pp. ISBN 91-7106-576-8

34. Fredrik Söderbaum and Ian Taylor (eds) *Micro-Regionalism in West Africa. Evidence from Two Case Studies.* 2006. 32 pp. ISBN 91-7106-584-9

35. Henning Melber (ed.), *On Africa – Scholars and African Studies.* 2006. 68 pp. ISBN 978-91-7106-585-8

36. Amadu Sesay, *Does One Size Fit All? The Sierra Leone Truth and Reconciliation Commission Revisited.* 2007. 56 pp. ISBN 978-91-7106-586-5

37. Karolina Hulterström, Amin Y. Kamete and Henning Melber, *Political Opposition in African Countries – The Case of Kenya, Namibia, Zambia and Zimbabwe.* 2007. 86 pp. ISBN 978-7106-587-2

38. Henning Melber (ed.), *Governance and State Delivery in Southern Africa. Examples from Botswana, Namibia and Zimbabwe.* 2007. 65 pp. ISBN 978-91-7106-587-2

39. Cyril Obi (ed.), *Perspectives on Côte d'Ivoire: Between Political Breakdown and Post-Conflict Peace.* 2007. 66 pp. ISBN 978-91-7106-606-6

40. Anna Chitando, *Imagining a Peaceful Society. A Vision of Children's Literature in a Post-Conflict Zimbabwe.* 2008. 26 pp. ISBN 978-91-7106-623-7

41. Olawale Ismail, *The Dynamics of Post-Conflict Reconstruction and Peace Building in West Africa. Between Change and Stability.* 2009.52 pp. ISBN 978-91-7106-637-4

42. Ron Sandrey and Hannah Edinger, *Examining the South Africa–China Agricultural Relationship.* 2009. 58 pp. ISBN 978-91-7106-643-5

43. Xuan Gao, *The Proliferation of Anti-Dumping and Poor Governance in Emerging Economies.* 2009. 41 pp. ISBN 978-91-7106-644-2

44. Lawal Mohammed Marafa, *Africa's Business and Development Relationship with China. Seeking Moral and Capital Values of the Last Economic Frontier.* 2009. xx pp. ISBN 978-91-7106-645-9

45. Mwangi wa Githinji, *Is That a Dragon or an Elephant on Your Ladder? The Potential Impact of China and India on Export Led Growth in African Countries.* 2009. 40 pp. ISBN 978-91-7106-646-6

46. Jo-Ansie van Wyk, *Cadres, Capitalists, Elites and Coalitions. The ANC, Business and Development in South Africa.* 2009. 61 pp. ISBN 978-91-7106-656-5

47. Elias Courson, *Movement for the Emancipation of the Niger Delta (MEND). Political Marginalization, Repression and Petro-Insurgency in the Niger Delta.*2009. 30 pp. ISBN 978-91-7106-657-2

48. Babatunde Ahonsi, *Gender Violence and HIV/AIDS in Post-Conflict West Africa. Issues and Responses.* 2010. 38 pp. ISBN 978-91-7106-665-7

49. Usman Tar and Abba Gana Shettima, *Endangered Democracy? The Struggle over Secularism and its Implications for Politics and Democracy in Nigeria.* 2010. 21 pp. ISBN 978-91-7106-666-4

50. Garth Andrew Myers, *Seven Themes in African Urban Dynamics.*2010. 28 pp. ISBN 978-91-7106-677-0

51. Abdoumaliq Simone, *The Social Infrastructures of City Life in Contemporary Africa.* 2010. 33 pp. ISBN 978-91-7106-678-7

52. Li Anshan, *Chinese Medical Cooperation in Africa. With Special Emphasis on the Medical Teams and Anti-Malaria Campaign.* 2011. 24 pp. ISBN 978-91-7106-683-1

53. Folashade Hunsu, *Zangbeto: Navigating the Spaces Between Oral art, Communal Security And Conflict Mediation in Badagry, Nigeria.* 2011. 27 pp. ISBN 978-91-7106-688-6

54. Jeremiah O. Arowosegbe, *Reflections on the Challenge of Reconstructing Post-Conflict States in West Africa: Insights from Claude Ake's Political Writings.*
2011. 40 pp. ISBN 978-91-7106-689-3

55. Bertil Odén, *The Africa Policies of Nordic Countries and the Erosion of the Nordic Aid Model: A comparative study.*
2011. 66 pp. ISBN 978-91-7106-691-6

56. Angela Meyer, *Peace and Security Cooperation in Central Africa: Developments, Challenges and Prospects.*
2011. 47 pp ISBN 978-91-7106-693-0

57. Godwin R. Murunga, *Spontaneous or Premeditated? Post-Election Violence in Kenya.*
2011. 58 pp. ISBN 978-91-7106-694-7

58. David Sebudubudu & Patrick Molutsi, *The Elite as a Critical Factor in National Development: The Case of Botswana.*
2011. 48 pp. ISBN 978-91-7106-695-4

59. Sabelo J. Ndlovu-Gatsheni, *The Zimbabwean Nation-State Project. A Historical Diagnosis of Identity and Power-Based Conflicts in a Postcolonial State.*
2011. 97 pp. ISBN 978-91-7106-696-1

60. Jide Okeke, *Why Humanitarian Aid in Darfur is not a Practice of the 'Responsibility to Protect'.*
2011. 45 pp. ISBN 978-91-7106-697-8

61. Florence Odora Adong, *Recovery and Development Politics. Options for Sustainable Peacebuilding in Northern Uganda.*
2011, 72 pp. ISBN 978-91-7106-698-5

62. Osita A. Agbu, *Ethnicity and Democratisation in Africa. Challenges for Politics and Development.*
2011, 30 pp. ISBN 978-91-7106-699-2

63. Cheryl Hendricks, *Gender and Security in Africa. An Overview.*
2011, 32 pp. ISBN 978-91-7106-700-5

www.ingramcontent.com/pod-product-compliance
Lightning Source LLC
Chambersburg PA
CBHW080210300326
41934CB00039B/3442